Yorkshire Terriers

by Julie Murray

Abdo Kids Jumbo is an Imprint of Abdo Kids
abdobooks.com

abdobooks.com

Published by Abdo Kids, a division of ABDO, P.O. Box 398166, Minneapolis, Minnesota 55439.

Printed in the United States of America, North Mankato, Minnesota.

102025

012026

Photo Credits: AdobeStock, Alamy, Getty Images, Shutterstock, Thinkstock

Production Contributors: Teddy Borth, Jennie Forsberg, Grace Hansen
Design Contributors: Candice Keimig, Julia Line

Library of Congress Control Number: 2025936494

Publisher's Cataloging-in-Publication Data

Names: Murray, Julie, author.

Title: Yorkshire terriers / by Julie Murray

Description: Minneapolis, Minnesota : Abdo Kids, 2026 | Series: Dogs | Includes online resources and index.

Identifiers: ISBN 9798384907541 (lib. bdg.) | ISBN 9798384908241 (ebook) | ISBN 9798384908593 (read-to-me ebook)

Subjects: LCSH: Yorkshire terrier--Juvenile literature. | Yorkie (Dog breed)--Juvenile literature. | Toy dog breeds--Juvenile literature. | Dogs--Juvenile literature. | Dogs--Behavior--Juvenile literature. | Animal behavior--Juvenile literature.

Classification: DDC 636.7--dc23

Table of Contents

Yorkshire Terrier

Yorkshire terriers are also known as "Yorkies." Yorkies are small in size but have big personalities!

Yorkies were first **bred** in Yorkshire, England, in the 19th century. This is where their name comes from. Yorkies were bred to catch rats in **mills** and **mines**.

Yorkshire
England
Europe
N
W
E
S

Yorkies are the smallest **terrier breed**. They stand 7 to 9 inches tall (17.8-22.9 cm) and only weigh between 5 and 7 pounds (2.3-3.2 kg).

Yorkies have a long, silky coat. Their hair is often **blue** and gold or blue and tan in color. Their ears are upright and alert.

Yorkies often have the hair on their head tied into a topknot. This keeps the hair out of their eyes. Some owners give their dogs a puppy cut instead. It is shorter and easier to manage.

Topknot
Puppy cut

Grooming

Yorkies need regular grooming. If their hair is kept long, they should be brushed daily. Baths and regular ear and teeth cleanings are important too.

Exercise

Yorkies have a lot of energy! They need daily exercise to keep them out of trouble. A fenced-in area is a great place for them to run and play.

Personality

Yorkies are smart dogs. They can sometimes be **stubborn** and hard to train. They also tend to bark a lot.

Yorkies are loving too! They enjoy cuddling next to their owner. They make great family pets.

More Facts

- Yorkies do not like temperatures that are too hot or too cold. They can wear a jacket if it's too cold outside.

- Yorkies have a long lifespan. They can live to be 16 years old!

- The American Kennel Club officially recognized the **breed** in 1885.

Glossary

blue – a black coat color that looks almost grayish or silver.

bred – developed over time for a certain purpose.

breed – a particular type of animal.

mill – or textile mill, a factory that processes materials into yarn, fabrics, and other textile products.

mine – a pit or tunnel from which minerals (as coal, gold, or diamonds) are taken.

stubborn – hard to handle, convince, or move.

terrier – any of several breeds of dogs. Terriers are small, lively dogs that were originally bred to drive animals from their holes.

Index